A Place Where Runaways Hide

A PLACE WHERE RUNAWAYS HIDE

MICHAEL TOBIAS

Copyright © 2016, Michael Tobias
All rights reserved.

ISBN-13: 978-0692662496
ISBN-10: 0692662499

In loving memory of my mama,
the first poet I ever knew.

Contents

Prelude	11
Runaways	12
Metamorphosis	14
Una Oda a Tus Ojos	15
Beach House	16
Studies in You	17
Concerning Stars	18
The Devil Rests His Hat	19
Ferris Wheels	21
The Man Who Mistook You	23
Lawns Under Stars	24
Let's Lay Low in the Moonlight	25
Una Oda a Tus Caderas	27
Fleeing Through Pines	28
To the Last Remaining Poets	29
Maliva	30
After Hours	31
Interlude	33
Just a Reminder	34
The Potter	35
At Your Doorstep	36
Getting Night to Bare Her Shoulders	38
Your Mother	40
Crucifilia	41
Una Oda a Tus Nariz	42
Mysticism	43
Orpheus	44
1/05 NYC	46
Descanso	47

Prelude

I didn't know I was asleep
until I saw that shoulder of yours,
bare and freckled.
My waking
wasn't quite like eyes opening.
It was more like a beetle
becoming aware of the moon.

Runaways

Close your eyes,
but don't let the serpent lull you with his song.

Let's make a run for it—
leap the chainlink fences of neglected lawns.

Leave the molcajete with her broken heart.
Leave the dented ladle with his hidden dreams.

Hurry, let's move quickly
past the lurks of lonely homes.

(They're just late wives, afraid of the dark,
afraid of how it ticks a second longer than ours.)

Come, little Lamia, hide with me in the grass,
and let's kiss in that orphan's jealous glow.

Let's forget our childhoods.
Let's imagine some treehouse for our kids.

Eternity simmers in a stew of stars
above the quiet startle of dust and dreams,

and somewhere on the other side
of a greedy mouth

a yawn of godless breath
creates new eyes to awe at nothing—

unless they're mine, staring into yours,
the suns perched upon the tired stones.

Metamorphosis

Like any force of nature
you are nearly indescribable, and yet
you try to imitate the clay,
trying to be sturdy, simple, and still.
But you are not indigenous.
You are the cosmic testament
of the dead poet's odes.
You wait at the foothill of Ovid's gods,
taunting them to curse you
as they did poor Daphne.
But they will not answer,
and you will not become a tree.
You must dip your toes into that sea within you.
As you descend forget your body
until every inch of you dines with turquoise.
The trout will dress you in their scales
as the frogs fill the air with tempered grief.
This is the magic you always wanted,
cool and slow and giving.
Succumb to its gentle touch.
Float away from heavy skin
until you're tip-toed on the sleeper's precipice,
about to go where nothing measures time.
That's where you'll find me
attending a sort of hatter's tea,
relishing each good and fleshless thought.

Una Oda a Tus Ojos

Fresh skin and freckled faces
make me coo like nicotine,

but blackberry eyes
in the orbits of your grim and sallow face,

sad as they may look,
cold and haunted as they may be,

wake me like a dusty snort of bliss.

Beach House

The second story windows contemplated the sea
while the bottom floor—drenched in dusk—
coddled our shadows like a hearth.

You said, *If you think about it,*
all of nature is one big hour glass
that slowly pours whatever souls are made from.

I unbuckled my belt,
and then laid you down on the sand.
I wanted to exonerate my father's sins with you
       before my time was up.

We came to like waxing moons—
more aware, more ripened than wrung.
It was the kind of thing that reminds me

of the first moment I understood you.
She wants to die among the leaves.
She knows nothing of stones.

Studies in You

You lay in the arms of Nietzsche's books,
giving him what soft is left in you.

You pull your braid of hair
as if it were a delicacy for those little hands.

I'm happy to watch you study,
how you become a swan in a pond of knowledge.

And I'm happy to interrupt—
sundering the book away to kiss you.

The stargazers watch you from a distance,
but I've been held in the orbit of your magnitude,

seen your landscapes singe with dawn,
experienced the epochs of a single breath.

I have felt the helplessness of continuously falling.
I have felt the mercy of never drifting into dark.

Concerning Stars

A chorus of ghosts sing
work songs as they march,
unaware that milliseconds mingle
in their masks of light.
Perhaps Mozart startled awake
when he heard them.
Why couldn't there be something more
pleasant in their murmur?
When skin leaves skin
there's a howl between the pores—
how could there not be?
It's just like how the black aches
between the glints of roars.

The Devil Rests His Hat

You looked lonely, silhouetted by the light,
and bare with a body so small.

Your skin perked and wanted
before I kissed the birthmark on your thigh.

I placed you on a makeshift altar
where I took your breasts as sacrament:

forgive me, I know not what I do,
for I am more flesh and blood than spirit.

I don't know when I dipped into an ether,
the decadent nothing,

but I felt deniable, simply discontinuous,
like a stone that could've been a pear.

The bickering neighbors woke me,
and looking for a friendly gesture

I wrote a poem
in the back of your linguistics book—

nothing profound, really,
just a few dirty syllables about your neck,

and a sad line about the moon.
      Nothing sentimental—
      Never sentimental—

So you shouldn't think I love you.
It was just something to do

while I waited for you to wake.

Ferris Wheels

I can't imagine a time so dark
we'd ever forget the wild of those colored lights.

We strolled along the empty arcade
as the workers whispered in their coves,
unsure of where to lose oneself in sleepy Roanoke.

    —there's an elegance to solitude.

I jotted down the five words in my journal,
and you frowned at my distraction.
But then I kissed you,

and I could see your irises catch the moment
like spiderwebs of light.
This is being young. I said to no one.

This is being alive! I yelled as I tried to swing
around a lamp like lithesome Mr. Kelly.
Only, I flung around to find you missing.

I remember feeling sick
from eating too much cotton candy.
I remember not wanting you to know.

In my mind there is only the dark of hillsides
as the spinning lights dip behind them.
What was said when we reached the top?

All I know is that the abandoned park,
glamorous in the glow of amber bulbs,
made me wish that I could start again.

The Man Who Mistook You

I suffered through his small talk:
weather, always weather,
and the status of his occupation.
He mumbles. Speaks a little too fast
like he's trying to dry his plume of dew.
He hums as he stares at strangers. Why is that?
Do you love him for his gentle eyes,
or do you love him for his peckish lips?
He's charming like a dinner chime—
dependable but jarring—
and isn't that what you always wanted?
He mentioned nightmares
where sparrows kept pecking at his eyes,
but he never talked about you.
Although he did mention autumn,
which reminds me of you,
the bare trees trembling
like your legs
when innocence left your skin.
I was going to remark about a family,
migrants, you know the sort,
but before I could speak
the birds had already diminished him.

Lawns Under Stars

I stood—a deathless boy
as if I were James Dean
on that observatory lawn,
loitering beneath withering suns
and heavy nothings.
We had nowhere else to go
when the fickle sky crumbled
into burning rocks.
I would've ran home,
but you held me, laughing coldly
from your strawberry throat.
We let stars possess our blood
as satanic cadences melodized
into gentle birdsongs.
You said, *isn't this grand, isn't this lovely?*
I thought you meant the pensive sky,
but you were fascinated
with us, laid out on green,
defying our destinies, hands held,
dreaming of places we'll never go.

Let's Lay Low in the Moonlight

We'll wait behind the wood rot,
light a lantern in the ribs,

let it yearn, let it want,
like the smallest jitter in the cold.

Through fixed droplets in a photo
sunlight undresses herself into broken hues.

The album reveals a quiet history of the residents;
why do we only photograph the good times?

Pressed flowers wait to bloom from yellow pages,
but man's failures are heavier than blooms—

what kind of school girl picked
these peonies for what kind of day?

The dry petals remind me of cicadas.
Having once recited odes to the languid air,

they've eloped from their bodies
to become melancholic fairies.

Are those the main street carolers I hear?
Or is it the Wind returning to the block
he left when Ovid made him famous?

No, it's just a mutt with his same old tale:
food, food, never enough to tire this old boy
of searching for a master.

On the walls needle-work of verses irk me—
empty alms for the kind-hearted dead.

It's why you should write your psalms in ashes
to wash away when the moon is red.

Am I demonic by the flames?
If so, put em out. Then kiss my limpid lips.

I'll only need the moon for love,
and to read your palms
as if they could end the endless day.

Una Oda a Tus Caderas

If I ever write a love song,
it will be with my tongue on your hips.

Every inch of your dark skin
will be full of rewrites

until the gooseflesh on your tan lines
makes me float with dissonant joy.

Fleeing Through Pines

We were once black furred wolves,
fleeing through pines
toward winter's dark mouth,

mocking the wooden ravens
who clod through snow
to hide from constellations.

Danger haunted each pine,
but we were drunk on moonlight,
taunting the eyes that stalked us.

In a pale clearing,
you asked, *Wouldn't it be romantic
to die beneath the stars?*

But morning came before death.
We woke in a treeless acre,
knowing this was not our promised land.

To the Last Remaining Poets

Do any of you still pen poems about love?
I think you should be attuned to your romantic fevers
rather than looking for pathos in your pillows.
We are persimmons, grainy and unsavory,
but our desires may make us appetizing yet.
I believe the crickets need assurances
that we are still opining with deep merlots
of honey-thick desire. They need to know.
Otherwise, we may see one parade
his vest of apricots to steal the moon away,
leaving us staggered by our darkened window panes.

Maliva

I'm an anemic boy
with a mind of interstellar sounds,

a bokeh of static and stars,
adolescent odes to your boundless soul—

the memory of indigo
that radiates behind your eyes.

Put a leash around my neck,
and I'm yours, always yours,

here, for you to toss
when you're bored of my lovesick mouth,

here, spinning the brittle hay
into strands of gold,

here, dead below the leaves,
conspiring to blossom into spring.

After Hours

Nat King Cole serenades the bare night
as I waltz through our kitchen,
cleaning pots, feeling dizzy, feeling grand.

Re-runs of *I Love Lucy* whine on the set—
dressed as a bull she mocks Ricky
for being such a dope.

Note: I've been needing to sleep in.
Note: I've been dreaming of envious plums.

Empty matryoshka dolls laugh
from the rafters of a studio:
look at how that knife cuts through tin!

Note to my younger self:
all my good shirts no longer fit me.

Are books good anymore?
I've been meaning to ask Ravi.
He's always reading to his bedridden father.

Now that I think about it,
I'll be needing fresh lilies for the wake.

Interlude

There are tears in your eyes—
where are we and what was said?
I just remember trains.
It was something about the migrants
that made you cry.
Seeing something no one ever sees,
this is the moment I fell in love with you.

Just a Reminder

Did you remember to water the plants?
It's the only part of the day
they enjoy as they sit on the sill,
longing for fields they've only seen in books.

They already forgive your bewilderment too much—
how you never know the right amount
to quench their thirst.

I read they favor Mozart in the evening.
Or was it the chimes of starlight?
Does it matter when all they hate is a silent room?

If I return to find them dead, I will leave you.
And that would be like you,
ignoring the only thing that brings me joy.

You'd rather trace those evocative lips
with juicy crimson, daydreaming of homes
with well-kept lawns.

Yes, I always think about my plants—
how you never know the right amount
to quench their thirst.

The Potter

Hands like loaves, hands like thunderheads,
hands like bookends on Umberto's shelf,
hands like tombstones at the edge of Eden.

They channel the memories in my sinews
the way my grandmother hears the dead.

The potter once told me my heart isn't a heart.
She called it a cabbage:
a dance of blushes that feeds the soul.

*You must understand a woman's body
is a perfect composition of lines*, she says,

*the conviction of spine,
      the sovereignty of her hips,*

*the sly taper of her eyes
      that punctuates eternity.*

*But don't think of her as a hen for clever foxes,
      or a crown for a crippled king—*

*she's a boy without maps and swords
      who like you wants for nests and pens.*

Feeling fed, forgetting the time,
I fell asleep on her breast.
And I didn't dream. I didn't dream. I didn't dream.

At Your Doorstep

Tonight this poet abandons caution,
crawling on your porch, begging for love.

Kerouac's hand is on your cheek,
praising your eyes, and you are just too happy

to give them to his words.
You devour his books,

as if they possess a cure for feeling lonely,
as if they could fix the past.

If my verbs could kiss you on the neck,
I'd have your thoughts.

If my nouns ran fingers through your hair,
I'd have your dreams.

If my last lines left tingles on your skin,
I'd have your soul.

The night is getting longer as we talk
without kissing,

and I'm afraid there's someone snooping.
Look at the feet blocking the lamplight

from the room next door.
What kind of man starts at those feet?

And will he serenade us
with the rhythm of his pacing

as he putters about the slenderness of time?
And what will he write of us

when he finally circles to his desk
to scare the crows from barren fields?

Getting Night
to Bare Her Shoulders

As we ascended the small hill
to the crowded view
of sodium lights disguised by mist

I kept looking at your olive skin,
jealous of the men before me,
wondering if you taste like sour nectarines.

You can't seem to shake those last drops of grief
from your Glenlivet eyes—
I want to see the look in them as I confess my wild

to your thighs, telling them how as a boy
I bottled the blushes of tabernacle girls
as counselors prayed we'd unwrap our souls of lust.

I confess that I waited too long
to have that something in my life—
whatever you have with what's his name,

your little wind-up husband
who forgets his cues to kiss you on your neck.
By chapter ten of this drama,

he'll reveal he was once a wooden boy.
Good suspense until I shake myself of you.
The bulbs of your spine lead me nowhere

as I search for those eyes of frail parhelic halos.
I want you to show me what night revealed
when once I held her in my arms—

all those lullabies of butchered lambs,
singing of trails imagined
to lead us to some field of light.

Your Mother

I had to resist seducing your mother.
She has your basil eyes—

green irises that smolder in delicate cradles.
Around them: a sad poet's calligraphy.

I could've spent the night deciphering them
with my lips.

I bet she makes love the way a tide
slithers on a black rock.

I want to crucify her on my bones until we tremble
in your childhood room,

mourning the birds and fauna,
all of whom are too pure to share this world
with sinners like us.

Crucifilia

I hate being the butt of jokes
and feeling glum and bloated
from your greasy meals.
And look at you:
your grin is red from
second glasses.
Your eyes dim,
and they remind me of a
procession of hoods,
marching beneath
a burnt sky.
I can barely recall
your adolescent eyes,
the frosted irises
full of morning sun,
the dilated pupils
bearing the rosy end.

Una Oda a Tus Nariz

In our long glance
your eyes are nothing without the nose—
pebbles held in orbit by the sun-kissed spire
built for a queen beyond the philtrum.
In a better poet's poem,
written sometime when the moon
was just a wren's imaginary friend,
words existed to express
the simplicity of nostrils—
how they swell and clench
from the bow of cartilage
as you catch your breath from kissing.
Your heart is nothing without the nose.
Hear how each breath betrays
the ravenous aorta
as we try to liquesce into dreams of stars.
No se olvide de las rosas, says Pablo,
as he drinks your skin from the sea.
Roses are nothing without your nose:
disembodied of beauty, absolved of death,
waiting for your mind
to form the fragrance into chroma.
Too many times I've longed for you
just from your delectable sillage.
I have washed myself in the earth—
its soil, its tobacco, its rain.
Memorize my scent
so that the elements make you think of me.
It's the only way I can live forever.

Mysticism

I bet you can't get your fill of lazy girls—
it must be why you're starving, Bicho.

We shed our talismans
      to exonerate the spirit from our bones,
revitalizing some child within.
      Your skin glowed with a watery silver
as you laughed, shivering from a holy thought.
           Below the boards,
    restless refugees groaned for the end of times,
while I kindled flecks of dawn within your hips.
      The particles—
elongated through the glass of
          spacetime—
                collapsed into a singularity,
    and for some reason it reminded me
        of a Spanish girl singing through
        barrancas,
singing to soothe her misplaced soul.

Orpheus

We walked toward the coast
through spring-sprayed woods.
Past the trees, I imagined a shore
where you could tumble
with your dress billowing
like an incoherent jellyfish.
Tell me about the sea, you said.
What is there to say? It's the sea, I said,
worried we were walking inland.
I hated myself for not knowing.
When you noticed, you held my hand,
and my heart ached in an old way:
as a child it hurt at the sight
of old people, so transfixed,
so unfed, so ready for sleep.
We passed trees like trees from our youth,
and I panicked, thinking I wasn't me.
Tell me about the sea,
you said as you began to fall asleep.

I'm standing alone in a rainless storm
surrounded by fallen birds.
Their delicate blue bodies
remind me of jacarandas.
Is there someone to feed me some broth,
to generously offer some day-old bread?
Soon will be the foxes.
And I'll still be lost on the long walk home.

1/05 NYC

I woke up from a nightmare
where my family met me in dark hallways.

I woke up not knowing
that you had finally left us,

and I read your obit,
remembering our nights in Brooklyn:

you were young and naive,
and I was vicious.

We poisoned ourselves with vanity,
and then danced like children

to the moans of lonely crooners.

You were a firefly
I held with my teeth,

and now my tongue tingles
with the recollection of nimble quips

from your sardonic mind,
the fission of your thoughts

barely contained
by your amber eyes.

Descanso

I polished my shoes,
made the bed,
dusted the books and lamps,
and plucked my nose.

I left out nibbles for the cat,
checked the locks,
and peered at the empty street.

I read the good book
and said a prayer:
bless this home to carry-on.
It has to carry-on
for God knows how long.

Was there anything else I needed to do?
You would've reminded me.

I've been forgetting my nose as a boy,
forgetting my friends playing pirates in ravines,
forgetting how the sky raptured the open fields
when they turned to dust.

I've trimmed my nails,
holding the clippings in my palm—
still baffled by unknowable things.

When I looked in the mirror
for a moment I thought I caught a glimpse
of how I looked to you:

stubborn and proud
like a weathered home on stilts.

Then my red, baggy flesh
mesmerized all imagination:

there I am, undetermined,
but feeling blithe beneath my gut,

like how yellow must feel
when it leaves the monarch's wing

to meet the eyes of poets,
finally unburdening itself of secrets.

How does one become a tree?
I never learned how.

What seemed easy was growing roots.
But how does one become at peace?

I forgot to wind my watch.
That must be what's keeping me awake.

Should I read one last letter
to take me back to where I've always been?

Or is there someplace better,
waiting to be invented by our sorrow?

I'd like to visit there sometime.
Seems pleasant. Seems like everywhere

will have those big wooden signs:
"The Guilty Have a Home Here."

Into the crystalline calm I'll call your name,
and every molecule will answer with the sky,

renewing my gift to soar
without needing to peck at the worms below—

what did you used to say about the shapes of clouds?
Doesn't matter. Can't remember.
                      —It's time to sleep.

A big thanks to Chrysta Naron for editing this collection and helping me bring out my strongest. This collection also shares the talents of the photographer Eric Carroll and model Emma Blyth. Thank you for creating such an arresting image for the cover. Dad, thank you for giving me the wisdom to approach everything I do with discipline and a dedication to mastery. I owe everything to you and Mom for supporting my endeavors with your joy and enthusiasm.

Michael Tobias lives in the Echo Park neighborhood of Los Angeles. He executive produced *Buffering*, a comedy web series, which garnered official selections at Big Screen, Little Screen LA and the HollyWeb Festival. In 2015, Mr. Tobias scripted a pilot for a new series, *American Dynasty*, a family drama about how second-generation Asian-Americans define their stories and identities as part of the American dream.

This is his first poetry collection.

aplacewhererunawayshide.com

www.ingramcontent.com/pod-product-compliance
Lightning Source LLC
Chambersburg PA
CBHW032100040426
42449CB00007B/1149